BACKLASH
PRESS

A pioneering publishing house dedicated to creating intelligent, vivid books.

Established to inform, educate,

entertain and provoke.

Journal Five

Backlash Press
71 Goldstone Crescent, Hove, BN3 6LS
backlashpress.com
info@backlashpress.com

Book design: Rachael Adams
Cover photo: Tomas Georgeson
Fonts: Baskerville, Bree serif
Print and binding: IngramSpark

A Backlash Book
First published 2021
Reprinted 2024

ISBN: 978-1-9162666-7-4
Copyright © Gretchen Heffernan 2021
The moral rights of the contributors have been asserted

All rights reserved. No part of this publication may be reproduced, stored in a retrieval system or transmitted in any form or by any means, electronic, mechanical, photocopying, recording or otherwise, without permission of the copyright holder

Contents

Soramimi Hanarejima	5
María C. Domínguez	7
Gret Heffernan	9
Paul Ilechko	13
Jessica Lowell Mason	15
Naomi Wood	17
Emily Rose Miller	21
Gareth Culshaw	23
Rosamund Davies	25
Naomi Wood	27
Ruth Seavers	29
Carla Scarano D'Antonio	31
Patricia Walsh	33
Thomas Simmons	35
Tomas Georgeson	37
Carla Scarano D'Antonio	45
Claire Scott	47
Sally Gander	49
María C. Domínguez	51
M-A Murphy	53
Elaina Parsons	55
Patricia Walsh	57
Amanda Leal	59
Gareth Culshaw	61
Claire Scott	63
Ruth Seavers	65
Josh Nicolaisen	67
Nicole Winters	69
Jessica Lowell Mason	71

To be read as one narrative.

Soramimi Hanarejima

Petrified Thought

Once the fervor of catching up over dim sum has run its course, we lapse into a lazy silence. Each of us occasionally sipping what's left of our tea. Until she asks me if I'd like to see some old thoughts up close. Of course, I take her up on this rare opportunity to look at actual artifacts from the psychological past. I've worked with plenty of models and replicas, but seldom do I get to see the real thing, and when I do, it's usually behind glass.

We walk down streets drenched in summer heat, back to the gloriously air conditioned museum. After a stop at her office for her curator's gloves and a guest pair for me, we're in the stairwell, descending numerous flights, passing multiple basements, finally exiting into a warehouse-like expanse. She takes me deep into a maze of metal shelving units, striding briskly as though navigating to our destination by muscle memory. When we reach it, she mounts a rolling stepladder and removes a metal box from one of the shelves high above my head. Once she's standing on the floor again, she places the box on one of the ladder's steps and opens it. The inside is partitioned in a manner reminiscent of a bento box, each compartment occupied by a tangle of thoughts like a little knot of noodles. All of them are very old and very wrong—a mess of misconceptions that hideously extend from flawed assumptions.

Petrified Thought / 2

"Astounding," I murmur.
"Yes, quite astonishing the kind of thoughts people used to have."
"I know these are from a different time and all, but it seems ridiculous that they ever made sense."
"Want to try some?" she asks, her words more invitation than inquiry.
"Aren't they fragile?"

"No, these are thoroughly ossified and unlikely to get damaged, unless rigorously challenged."
"OK, I'll try not to question them."

We slip our hands into the soft, white gloves, and she picks up a bundle of thoughts about love. When she places it on my open palm, I think I'm in for some old-timey folklore about romance.

But no. The moment I wrap my mind around them, these thoughts lock my attention in a vice grip of beliefs about who can love whom and even who deserves love. The limiting perspective repulses me, but a moment later, in sweeps the intoxication of complete certainty—the total confidence that these beliefs are correct, part of the unequivocal order of the world.

Utterly exhilarating and deliciously comfortable, like being tightly snuggled up in voluptuously fuzzy air. I revel in it, clutching the railing of the stepladder as euphoria swirls within me. My sense of self wavers. Afraid the ecstasy will incapacitate me, I relinquish the antiquated thoughts.
"Wild, isn't it?" she says.
"Yes. We've come a long way."
"Though there's still a ways to go."

Petrified Thought / 3

But is there even a road to weaning ourselves off the pleasure of feeling right? Ideas come and go—instincts endure.

María C. Domínguez

What the Virus Gave Her

She began having conversations with herself during quarantine.
It didn't stop there, so she spoke

to the crows who visited her yard,
they chatted and shared their terrible secrets.

The trees eavesdropped, their leaves
silent, resting on branch-like chins.

She spoke to her cat and the cat spoke back
with its extensive eye vocabulary.

Ants parading near the kitchen sink
carried crumbs like love codes across a page.

The sun's warmth spoke to her, its lemony-yellow
tones pressed against her window pane.

The full moon a balloon without a child
pulling her close to earth.

When she was finally allowed outside her house
she forgot,

how the world and its creatures had offered her something
and asked for nothing back.

Gret Heffernan

Redneck IV

In my early memories, I am often drawing boats –
Nina, Pinta, Santa Maria – transformed by my imagination and box of crayons.
I was landlocked; there were waves in the grasses, the dust, the clouds, but no wild ocean.

For me, the ocean was mysterious, as was the cosmos, and, being a religious child, mysterious notions were rinsed, like the head of babes, in salvation. I learned how to tell stories about things I'd never seen.

I folded my drawings into small, palm-sized squares and stuck them inside my pillowcase. In the bowel of night,
I would rub the cloth over the squares of my fleet,
position them in an arrow and imagine myself as a living figurehead.

Hair tangled, the spray of salt, the escape of fate, and into civilization,
which I expected to behave as a chart of experience
that unfolded with each realm of possibility.

In my head, my measure of civilization grew, similar to the celestial sky that grows into its changing self as the boat traverses.

The distance seemed implicit, as did the pushing forward.
The ship pressing and moving through a force of untold depth.
All the necessary components of mythmaking.

We analyze a myth after it's been fixed into our narration
and it feels like a prophecy.

When I met my husband, twenty years later, we walked to the river of our

university town and spoke of boats and fell in love. Love happens inside the mysteries
you discover you've shared.

The secret of love is sharing a secret. Just like
the secret of manipulation is holding a secret ransom.

*

We create things.
All aspects of civilization extend
from this defining moment in our animals' history.
To create is what humans do, what we've always done,
and around the things we've created, we build our stories
so that the two are inseparable, interlaced hands.
Once released, our creation survives inside a story
that context makes
into a fluid being.

In this fluidity of truth, the story of dogma
has become the story of our expiration.

We recreate our truths by changing the context of our storylines
into tales that we can love.

The greatest unknown in anything is its love.
And, to hate is to irrationally fear the loss of something you love,
which could be a person, an idea, or your understanding of your place in the world. To love something is to make it erasable and our utmost fear is erasure. Humans do not want to feel erasure.

So, held ransom to our fear of obliteration, we create the conditions that guarantee it by insisting that consumerism is personal freedom, the mask for tyranny.

Our idea of freedom is also a fluid creature composed of language and delusion
and the rhythms that magnetize our preverbal devotion.

Where we translate our stories into the truths we want to maintain
rather than the truths that present themselves as real.
Such is the trickery of the story. The story can behave groundlessly –
it can make monsters from nothing,
saints from nothing as long as its translators use words
that embody emotions that trigger
the instinctive trappings of the current time.

Consume. Distrust. Powerless. Division.

What we say now we say for history.
Shorn of our choices.
Waver between defining moments.
Denuding. Most of us, sheep. Easily captive to distorted translation.

Because the pathway from experience to meaning to application
is so personal and subjective that speaking the same language
is secondary to what is being (or not being) understood.

We need to feel our words again. We need to access that
chamber locked in the preverbal dualistic universe
where words are musical, visual performances.

And language is a known
creature.

Paul Ilechko

Crucial Differences

The crucial difference being a memory of sound across
the surface   there was no color trapped within

the watery light that flowed like a ribbon across the mirror
flowed into the pure potential of a glowing morning

a monochrome morning that gradually blurred
and shimmered   as original silver alchemized to gold

it was a kind of love   trapped within the frame
of dawn   a burning time of regret for all of the predictable

divisions   the deviations from a true trajectory
full of vengefulness and swagger   of broken

lives no longer functional inside their misery
their provisional motion of branching and parting

all that remained was fear   a blatant manifestation
of a hidden grief that strived for decades

to burst into the visible   living outside the standard
structures of our commonly known humanity

leaving only a reconstruction of a nucleus   a race
of spinning electrons beyond the reach of any charge

the crucial difference is a liquid thread that pumps

and batters our lost capacity   dropping from

a pinnacle that may never be reclaimed   all drained
and lost   leaving behind a dry and withered

landscape   lacking any signifiers   a flatness of ice-flooded
fields that stretch away into the quiet unknown.

Jessica Lowell Mason

The Mad Card

We were the women
who would lose our children;
if for nothing else,
we were destined for that.

Our husbands, even those
we didn't know we had,
would pull
the combs out of our hands.

We would be silenced at the bus
stop: one word and the tiny
limbs that formed within us
would be yanked away.

We knew this spoken
and unspoken fact,
we knew the shock of the tug,
the weight of powerlessness;

We knew the consequences,
the wrangling, the mess of hearts,
but we couldn't help
but open our mouths.

We were to be introduced
to terror; the introduction

would prepare us
for more intimate encounters.
Midnight would make crescents
of us, position us fetally,
follow us with night
-visions of death.

If we leave, we will lose,
but how much?
Will he kill
our babes to makes us pay?

It's not gender alone
that makes a wounded lover
an eraser of the mother,
but the patterns constellate.

Our husbands will say,
if they cannot have us,
that we are unfit,
they will play the mad card.

We will be what we have been:
unfit wives
to husbands who will wipe us out
if we should leave.

I look out the window
for the lesbian menace,
but it acts as a mirror: I see you,
I see we are outnumbered.

Naomi Wood

The Gift

The gift is her asking me to unfasten
Her costume.
To watch the old stories burn
With their binding.

I thought I might become rain
At the site of so much tenderness.
Curling my spine the other way
To see myself for the first time.

The gift is being ripe again.
In full bloom through the seasons,
Its waking up after the longest winter.
It's cutting my hair so they couldn't climb it
To my thoughts.

My thin-king.
The crown
Hard won after being locked in the tower.

Turns out I had the key all along.
I'd swallowed it down with the taste of honey and marzipan
Still ringing on my lips
Like church bells.

The gift is her fingernails
In my skin
Five instruments to carve her name

Into my flesh
As I lose my breathe to speak it.
It's all the softness and rage
Poured out
And meeting the same river
As the typhoon keeps gathering speed.

Wave after wave
Forging new pathways in its wake
But the gift.
Is that
The soil is regenerating.
My flesh bears new blooms.

And she tastes each one
Like they are a rare and precious delicacy-
Fruit furred with gold.

We show each other the seams
Where we restitched our flesh
Tracing the lines with fingertips
And tongues.

The gift is memorising the details.
Swallowing the seeds
Like children hoping
The fruit tree will bloom
In our centre.

The gift is bleeding for ourselves again
Coughing up the medicine they fed us to
Regulate our trips to the moon.

But now we have made branches
Of our bodies and sails

From our skin.
And we water the ground
With hot showers for our dancing feet.

The gift is that here, locked away from the world
We can make a home anywhere.
The gift is that we can grow ourselves.

Emily Rose Miller

Spaces Between

The Space Needle towers above us where we lie in the grass—clean grass, not like grass back home with the itching and the bugs and the sand. This is urbanized grass, grass where the dirt stays neat and clean underneath unnaturally even, nearly-artificially verdant, blades. It's pretty, in a weirdly fabricated way.

It's just the opposite of you—wild hazel eyes and windswept hair you didn't bother to brush this morning. You're a sun's ray across my face, heating and glowing on my cheeks and maybe blinding me, just a little, but I don't mind because it's a privilege to bask in your sunshine. There are brown, cloud-shaped stains on your pants and one right below your knee looks like George Washington, so I point and laugh. And your smile, oh, the sight of your smile with your uneven teeth and freckled upper lip makes my stomach do an amateur pirouette and levitate like a lost balloon up to the top of the Needle. Tourists, there, peer over rounded railings to look at all the people lying in the too-perfect grass and laughing at each other with lovely, imperfect grins.

It's a cycle, this city—spinning around and around like the restaurant at the top of the Needle, like my buzzing around your shining aura. The rain fills the waves drive people to the monorail dries the rain on its windshield wets the tent-cities in the streets block the tourists move to 1st Avenue runs parallel to the Sound makes waves fill up with rain that inspires us, so. And my gaze draws back to you where your splayed limbs leave a haphazard silhouette in the grass. I think that if I could lay in that spot forever, with your shape around me, I could be happy.

I could stare at the way your eyes tilt down at the corners and feel how all of those itty details that make you you fill me with awe and maybe a little bit of indigestion because how could someone *not* worry about losing you? You're a whirlwind, and the question isn't *if* I'll lose you but when, kind of like the way I'll have to let Seattle go, too. But, like your everything, I'll carry its ever-bustling details with me, aching for just one more minute to close the spaces between us.

Gareth Culshaw

Consumption of the Mind
(Based on the short story, *Peasants*, by A.Chekhov)

The wind blew away the spring spider-webs
that spread across the fields. Doctor Ergunov
walked with his medicine bag. His feet were sore
from two hundred and seventeen days of work.
A cow watched him from a barn. Two children ran
around trying to catch up with adulthood.

Dr Ergunov opened his mouth to release a yawn.
One of his ears popped, and the sound of a horse and cart
woke up his skull. He let the traffic go by, tilting his head,
then he looked at the openness of farmland.
Birds flocked in huge numbers, rooks bent the sweet sound
of chirping, and a sky curved the earth.

The doctor waited a moment. His next patient was a man
of consumption. He knew the man's cough fed the air,
his lungs were capsized ships being eaten by microbes.
Each visit, Dr Ergunov prayed before he went into the house.
He placed a handkerchief by his mouth when talking
to the man, closed his eyes between sentences.

A farmer walked with his bull. A wild dog sniffed the road
as it lumbered towards the doctor. Its tail weighty as a hangover.
A cat sneaked between hedgerows. Two men trotted
on their horses. They were local thieves with shiny shoes,
clean shaven, and dusty hats to keep out the frost. They smiled
at the doctor. Looked down at him as hawks on prey.

Dr Ergunov squinted as he looked into the sun's soup.
His hands shook from onion skin cold. The knees he was born
with buckled on gradients, leg muscles groaned each morning.
A pheasant ran across his path, then flew away.
Dr Ergunov put down his bag. He felt the hole in his shoe,
and his foot peeped as a mole out of soil.

A blackbird sang from an ash tree. The doctor listened.
A blackbird sang from an ash tree. The doctor listened.
A blackbird sang from an ash tree. Dr Ergunov picked up
his bag. Walked towards the man's house with the steps
of a cheating lover going back home.

Rosamund Davies

Eye of the Beholder

The market smells of salt and spice and smoke and fat. The air is sweet with hot sugar, sour with sawdust and blood.

Wheels rattle on the cobbles, a pushchair weaves through the stalls, bearing a child, her gaze intent on shapes and colours streaming by on either side, just out of reach.

She stores them as pictures, for future reference – many of them pictures without captions, since she does not know the words for all the things she sees. Red, APPLES, yes, green, more green, red red red, orange ORANGE, little, purple, eat, yellow BANANAS one, two, three, more green, more yellow, more red, big red, brown, dirty, soft... gone... here, red pink, wet, close, there, another thing she can name –

'FISH' she yells.

The fish lies on a slab in front of her, level with her eyes. It is shiny and silent.

'Fish,' the child says again, pleased with her catch.

The inert body twitches. Its glassy eye stares into hers. She stares back.

Her mouth opens, as if in a question.

The fish's mouth opens too.

The child looks at the fish, the fish looks at her.

What is the word for this? For the moment when a picture looks back at you?

The question hangs between them, alive, electric. Neither has the answer. The moment expands, nameless, one second, two seconds, three seconds...

The fish's tail flaps very slightly then rests motionless on the slab.

'Fish' whispers the child.

The fish lies still.

Naomi Wood

Objects

I carry these objects with me
From place to place.
Fewer each time,
I'm paring back the dead weight.
I'm losing layers of threadbare tropes.

But each time I pack up
What's left of me
I know not everything goes
And a piece of me remembers
Midnight fleeing,
Five year old fingers
Clutching at straws

And neighbours
Who sent their children
Out into the night to carry

Our belongings across the road,
Piece by tender piece-
A blighted benediction.

You knew one more time
Would be too many and you
Packed up your heart, Mother,
In a suitcase meant for holidays
And we fled into the inky darkness

And we lived on shoestrings
Cos it was better than bottle tops
And we lived in so many
Makeshift situations
Cos anything is better
Than building bridges on a fracture.

I carry a tiny box of defiance
That seizes small things
In the face of having none

And every object is a tool
With which to build
Your own freedom
If you hold it the right way.

Ruth Seavers

The Beach

I don't remember details as I never really do but I remember not feeling what I was supposed to be feeling.

It was grey outside and you stood in my kitchen and asked me to walk to the beach with you. The one we used to drink on in summer evenings. You were nervous as you stood there but were careful not to hide this from me.

We walked in silence, the tension pregnant in the air as we moved. We passed the cemetery where we hid under the tree that day, where your lips were soft and mine. Silent in the after school still. Your sweetness knew no bounds that day.

As we walk, I think about those days in which I betrayed you. How malignant I had made everything. All twisted and gnarled and ugly. And how if it weren't for those days we wouldn't have today this day; today, walking towards the beach in silence. Towards your admittance of guilt.

I know those days are playing in your mind, too. Which image hurts you the most? I wonder. Was your imagination crueller to you than I had been?

I did not realise it at the time but telling you was self indulgent. All I had done was pass the cancer on to you and now it had grown into something terrible and far beyond both of us and now you, like me, were trying to extract it. But it was always growing. It would never really go away.

We walked along the dry stone wall, weeds bowing from the cracks and the ground begins to disappear under dirty sand.

I wanted to get there as fast as I could so I could experience an emotion I had never felt before. I knew what you were going to tell me. I saw it as soon as you walked into my kitchen. I almost felt sorry for it.

It was windy. The sand dunes dirty and hissing at our ankles, whispering and littered from being in such close proximity to urban life.

And then we stopped. And you turned. And it was moments like this, I think, where our innocence wore away like the dry stone we had just walked along. As we grew older I think these things made you bitter, like you sucked lemons in your sleep.

*

But in the wind you told me. Your face said the words I can't remember but meaning I recall. Like a movie in my head I can play over and over again. No sound. Just memory. Your lips moving against the salty damp wind from the shore.

I played it for weeks after, trying to make it hurt.

But right before you spoke, your eyes. Your eyes had this look in them. Which said maybe it was all my fault. Maybe if it wasn't for those days where I laid my skin bare against somebody else's, you wouldn't be looking at me and telling me this right now.

But right before you spoke; your eyes, they begged me to care.
And I didn't.

Carla Scarano D'Antonio

Balloon

The balloons swing in the blue sky, tied to white strings. They are in a bunch, held by a heavy stone on the ground.

Miriam chooses a Minnie Mouse, with a shiny pink ribbon between the black ears. The balloon-man ties the string to her wrist like a bracelet.

"Are you happy now?" her mother says, striding towards the girl's father, pulling Miriam behind her.

He is waiting at the entrance of the zoo.

Miriam hurries alongside. "Yes," she whispers.

"Have you got the tickets?" her mother asks looking at the girl's father.

He takes a long puff on the cigarette and stamps it out. "No. I didn't fancy queuing."

"You promised her the zoo." She points at Miriam. "You never keep your promises to her."

"Fuck you," he hisses.

Smiling Minnie hovers above the trees, soon a tiny dot in the dazzling light. Miriam stands, her head upwards, her wrist burning, a red line marking where the string was.

Patricia Walsh

Proper Job

Educated into badness, a probable discernment
Looking for arguments, having gone for the food
Singular persuasion goaded into action,
Counting the hours shorter into necessity.

Burning for sale, an errand perniciously
Cremated ambition at a cost of worth
Watering into distaste, the historic rising
Returning to the whole fitted cream.

Adopted liberally as ever, dead into preference
Sins falling on the siblings, hitting remorse
These tenuous creatures call from aged kilometres
Hovering over the scales, well rested and fed.

Broken for a song, the better to stand ground.
Gone after with a club, well into perception
The forty-hour week is still going to waste
Holding where none afforded, sated at last.

Signing in and out, only the necessary is seen
In praise of destination, never mind the journey
Picking through necessary positions, like so,
Hitting the right notes, unto us is given.

Fearing the gunfire, more so than the bullet
A pup with an attitude wasted over duty,
Borrowing perfection from a finished apogee

Entering into the quiet realms of the material.

Thomas Simmons

Old Sheet Music

She knew nothing of doom in this woven depth
She hungered for not even an atom of yeast
    She was sanctimonious of groveling

Dark but far from formless; crystalized and fantastic
Hovering, beaming without pride or understudies
    Lights placed in the vault to divide everything

Dominating the night; a sovereignty bestowed on
a synthesis of presence. She stuck her trust into it
    She reckoned it to her merit

The muscles in her neck foretold eschatological victory,
She surged into radiance; she knifed; levitated as a saint
    Overtop the glens and ripples, a tide rolling on

She was dwarfed yet secured by incorruptible fabric
Her taste was not her own. She didn't merge with it;
    Her calloused dervish was quilted

Her ribcage cracked at the doorway
Her lungs collapsed like a harpsicord
    She emitted splintering thrills

Tomas Georgeson

Aylesbury

It rained on this town from 84 to 96
A decade of drizzle
All through the streets
At night between the cobbles
With the beer dregs, like black ink
Or the forgotten blood
Of fleeing Stuart kings
Discovered hooded in an inglenook
With dogs and wards

Citadels of concrete
Climbed over those great old inns
Poured up when you wore bell bottoms
And for a while
Without damp stains, in perfect sun
Their vision almost struck a chord
More resonant than what had been knocked down
But not for long

One for the mayor
One for the clerks
One for old books

And somewhere, later
A Sam goody
A Beaties toys
A Tandy perhaps?
Shining thin promises

Into a downpour

The Manor

Waking in the east village
Wrapped in twenty year old sheets
A relic of our boyhood you kept
I roll in a funk of having to leave

Last night
Returning from the city at dusk
I pack, we eat in some Chinese cafe you know
Stupid delicacies which cost the earth
We split the bill and say goodbye
And guilt and doubt and weariness return

I know that time and distance
Have obscured what that place was
The Manor
Your old home
So that its being ours means nothing now
Accept to us
Again in this weird country
We are each other's proof

Of frost
Outside the beams and Jacobean oak
Like warm black stone
Cut into corridors
And rooms and antechambers
A hive of antiquity
Of wood smoke and your mothers lilies

Lit by shallow sun and hearth light
And us, as boys
Wild with hope

Norfolk Wedding day

Tiring salt soaked gulls
Slope out on the wing
And unfamiliar dunes
Flanking the broads
Make deep, unfathomable progress
More slowly than a lifetimes witness

Beyond white tops turn pink
Beneath the most oblique
And mesmerising evensun

And out and out and out
Until the turning of the globe
Makes night inevitable
And all of this is gone
Except for what is heard
And the prospect of those birds
Cawing in august dawn

Development Site, drawings by Tomas Georgeson

Carla Scarano D'Antonio

Bianca

From the top of the tree I can see chickens and geese scratching about in the backyard. My favourite hen, Bianca, is hiding behind a tyre leaning against a tree trunk. The cock is after her, his red neck shining, sweating, stretching high and gurgling. He smells the air searching for Bianca, jerks his small head, turning it one side and the other, his claws grasping the earth.

Hide Bianca, hide. Don't let him touch your snow-white wings, smear your back. But you can't fly. You can't hide in the trees like me. I can see how he corners you against the fence and hurts you, pecking and pricking. And I can't help you.

'Maria! Come down: time to go to church,' my mum says.

They closed their restaurant today, just today, for granddad's funeral. I don't want to see his wrinkled shiny neck again, his long nose and his hands like tongs grabbing me and holding me from the back.

Tomorrow they will be busier than ever. They won't look for me.

Maybe I can die falling from this tree, or need to find an even higher spot. The top of the house where we live and work, or the church tower, or the walls of the castle.

I nestle on the branch holding my knees and keep quiet.

Claire Scott

Third Grade

The teacher taps me on the shoulder
time for another trip to Mrs. Gardener
who asks a lot of questions
is your mother home after school
what did you eat for dinner last night
who leans over her desk and looks at me
with soft green eyes, glistening lipstick
and upper arms that jiggle as she writes
her office smells of lilac

I am scared of her, scared of a wrong answer
should my mother have been home
does it count if she locks herself in her room
and won't answer when I knock
is Spaghetti O's with burnt lima beans
a real dinner if my mother doesn't eat
only drinks endlessly from a glass with ice
and throws noodles at the cupboards
clapping if they stick

This time she reads questions from a Test
I know it is Serious
I look at my lap when I answer
my school uniform bunched at my knees
my saddle shoes tapping the legs of the chair
I think I am doing pretty well until she asks
if I count church bells when they ring
I know one answer is right

the other means I am crazy

Mrs. Gardner smiles, encouraging
her pencil poised like a guillotine

Sally Gander

rhizomes of memory

rhizome *[rahy-zohm]* noun: botany
a root-like subterranean stem, growing horizontally along or under the ground and producing roots and leaves
*

each day you look out from your lockdown window at the roof of the neighbouring house where moss grows in a green smudge down the slates. Each day the sky is different, but today a white dove flies across a pale sweep of cloud
*

the vast open sky above the Nevada desert, your children staring out the car window at the ribbon of heat-hazed tarmac leading to Death Valley. *The Velvet Underground* is playing through the speakers
*

your then lover on stage playing the saw, his bow sliding through serrated teeth. Some in the audience glance to each other, their eyes asking, *Is this real?*, the ethereal vibration filling the space as bubbles rise from nowhere. The magic of this moment is lost on the saw player, he is too deep in the music, the bubbled tent suspended in held breath
*

a bell tent perched on a cliff top. You clamber down rocks to reach the beach and the unpredictable sea, where the tide rushes in to gulp up your bag. A naked man runs through the surf to save it but your dress is lost, so you climb back to your tent in your bikini. Later you imagine a dolphin shimmying through waves in the dress
*

identical dresses with frills and yellow spots, you and your friend crammed into the changing room to laugh at your reflection. You are both university lecturers, but in that moment you are 1980s disco queens
*

the Queen on mugs, plates, tea towels, china thimbles. Your grandmother is a royalist and wears a royal blue shift dress for special occasions. She has black hair until the day she dies, and black hair sprouting from her pale chin

*

your daughter's hair shimmering in the holiday sun, natural honey highlights that you plait into narrow strands. She holds up her fingertips where a transparent crab sits patiently as you reach for your camera. The framed photograph is a mere lean away as you write this now

*

photographs of Sicily, the lush Catania courtyard in the Monastero di San Nicolò l'Arena, your feet aching from a day walking the fevered streets, this gloriously baroque building now home to throngs of university students. It will be a long time before you're surrounded by such enquiring young minds again. You are still waiting

*

your enquiring mind a never-ending slide show, a multitude of classrooms, houses and gardens, holidays and celebrations, open books, journal pages, roads, fields, forests, landscapes, towns and cities, airports, train stations, bus terminals, hotels, Airbnbs, dinners with friends, coffees, cakes, family meals. And now, isolation conversations within the window frame of your laptop or mobile phone

*

your mobile phone a list of people you love. People you miss and want to hold. They all have their own window of memory and imagination to quicken the day, and you feel joy for this.

María C. Domínguez

Come soon, my love

My dear absent one,

we wait for you.
The sun and I.
        The cat.
                Your remote.
The pigeons you defend; the carpets expecting your feet.
The bottles of water, your mugs and ivory comb.

My hands and shoulders, empty, shaking.
My face which doesn't reflect,
covered in a thick mist.

What can I say,
that everything has remained as it was?
No.
The unfaithful objects have moved.
Some furniture has been carted off to another home
Your drawings and words closer to the ground, you know that for sure.

The world outside has flipped.
The four Horsemen of the Apocalypse
are plundering our earth, you said.
No wars yet or hunger, well maybe yes,
hunger for what we had before.

I covered the terrace with a new floor. Grey smoke, it reflects the warmth.
There's a solar light, a globe that goes on whenever it senses movement,

I think of it as you. So close I can almost feel
your breath in my ear as you tell me

you're the one who's waiting.
But I wait for you.

M-A Murphy

Flowers

Lockdown is making me draw so many flowers.
All I can think about are flowers.
It is the dead of winter here in Treaty Six Territory (Edmonton).

Everything is asleep.
All I can think about is spring.
G R O W T H.

Roots.

I dream about spring.
I dream about flowers.
I dream about community
And being together again.

Elaina Parsons

Skinny Twenty Something

Bones and olives
Competitive vocals
Loud vocals
Beauty-marks that shatter into
Moles—thick and murky tailspins
Nestling into my thick bones again
I love the attention.
Tendons, so Italian,
Veins ripe with suspicion.
My aches so Italian,
My heart, so Depeche,
Hurried.
My breath wielding
Paring knives over
Thick masculine figs
As the fat girl above whispers in my ear: eeeaaaat.
But I want to be thin, strong,
Like Madonna
Silk flowers dominate my space,
Scissors curl ribbons all over
My Madonna-shaped face.
Voices bake up
Hate,
Fear,
For the young girl
Who sees right,
Straight through
Boy-made hogwash.

Forty-one words
Required.
In the middle —
Full of Grace.
The lord is with thee.
I want to world to see
Me.

Patricia Walsh

Disinformation

The silk informancy links to the blockades
Likely to come true, a synthetic music
If ever doing drugs, catch-all not surprising
The implicating residue rolls off its back
Loved on probation, sank into the fold.
The distanced appointments like never made
Hot to the touch, cancelling the moment
Ordinary-level practicalities forewarned
Good as misbegotten, the times straitened
Clear as double-glazing on the common street.
The idiotic ambition, corralled into descencion
Before the locking of doors to go readily
Hiding behind the inklings of solid reckoning
Working through presence of an angered time
Weird to a point, not always a good thing.
Declarations of love now striking false
What goes on, remains on, staying the same
Different though it is, the changing man
Chocolate weaknesses fuel the heated wire
Watching the informants with due carelessness.
Thinking over the odds at night, remaining in light
The sound of the manufactured seated still
Rolls off its husk, a conscionable decision
Looked at wisely, good as married since
Prizes for guessing, suited and booted.

Amanda Leal

Hatton Highway

On Saturday night, we begin driving west, navigating
our trail through Belle Glade, where the streetlamps stand
arms length apart, spacing further from one another
until they disappear, the darkness a heavy brow
on the windshield, as my boyfriend peers over the dirt road,
Hatton Highway an open mouth stretched before us. He remarks
that he has never seen the sky so empty,
as I roll down my window and let the wind gush
in the body of the car like a tide,
handfuls of stars studded to the stratum above, purples
like bruising, hazy clouds that circumvent
the snow moon like a belly button.
I laugh and tell him, *You have never been
so wrong.* The car crackles to a stop over the gravel, headlights
carving deep shadows on the guard rails, a chorus of bullfrogs
chirping alongside baby alligators, and across a corn field
miles long, divided by flat glass canals, headlights
drift slowly as ants on their hill. As my own car dims
like a candle blown out, I realize how easily
I could no longer exist, how quickly my screams
could flatten. Suddenly, I remember the story of Sydney Loofe,
her date who disassembled her body with a table saw,
above the kneecaps, below the pelvis, her hands
chiseled free of the carpal bones, her torso intact
within the trash bag, the skin of her breasts macerated,
the accelerated decomposition along the unpaved roads
within Clay County, as the Earth reclaimed her life.

Now, I watch my boyfriend steady the telescope, auburn hair
at his freckled neck, his figure perched on the guard rail,
his rounded hands thick as mitts that twirl
the silver dials of the eyepiece, the precision
of his movements, his fingers trailing the shoulder
of the telescope. I remember at once the tenderness of his hands,
his flat palm to my upper back only hours ago, pressing me
to the mattress with certainty. He pushed up into my body
as though poring for what he knew was there,
and with my face to the linens, I rocked with him,
in the white noise of my own breath, his weight upon my scapula,
my anchor to this world. Moving to him now,
my trust defines itself, as concrete as the breaking cries
of the bullfrogs. I join his side on the guard rail,
the silver sluice below us, sea grape trees
the color of machinery in the dark, his hand to my inner thigh
as he pulls me closer, his lips to my temple,
the stars glittering on the surface of the eyepiece,
miracles pooled like tadpoles in the canal,
the improbability of our tandem, our resolution of trust.

Gareth Culshaw

Ivan

(Based on the short story, *The Death of an Official* by A Chekhov)

When Ivan was a small boy his father beat him until the belt
could take no more. Sometimes Ivan stuffed straw down
his pants on his way home from school, knowing
one wrong word or mistake in the house, and the belt would
slither out of its trouser loops. Ivan stood as if in a breeze everyday.
One teacher placed a book on the young boys head told Ivan
to hold his hands together, then breath slowly.
Soon enough the book fell down and Ivan ran out crying.
He ran to his grandfather's home as the belt there was not as thick.
At harvest time Ivan helped with the crops. His egg-shell
hands carried tools, pushed a wheelbarrow, and once dropped
a scythe on the floor as his father carried potatoes.
That night, Ivan sat at the dinner table with an empty plate.
One winter time the family was full of cold. Ivan coughed
at dinner shooting green phlegm onto his father's food.
For months later Ivan had poker burns on his bum. Some say
when his father died Ivan picked up the coffin and the handle broke.

Claire Scott

Hope Springs Absurd

Things turn out for the best
could have fooled me who just lost her job,
was evicted by a seedy landlord,
and now lives under a cardboard box near I-80
it all happens for a reason
there can be no reason for a black man
unable to breathe, for a trans woman covered
in bruises, for a Mexican boy locked in a cage
miles from his frantic mother

Words of bright-eyed optimists
floating on fluffy clouds in La La Land
we are all in God's hands
living happily in their myopic world
putting a positive spin on climate change, on health care
everything will be OK
while the rest of us eye pills and tall buildings
Ativan days, Lunesta nights
attitude is a choice
haunted by dreams of disaster, fires licking our homes,
good old Joe losing, relentless COVID, ruinous medical bills,
pent-up kids refusing to learn, no paper towels or rice
until we wish we too believed
we are not given more than we can handle

Ruth Seavers

the family

when isobel fell
we promised we'd never fight in front of the children again

but then sure you started talking about last christmas
with my father
and the slip of it came through my tongue like his whisky did
and before i knew it i'd followed

the linen starched, i stared at your sweaty furrow,
haggard bees, nasty from the farm swarm you

and i quelled before you did,
you bastard

and the lake that surrounds us lapped and licked our heels
as i took the children to bathe
in antagonism

Josh Nicolaisen

Just You and Me

When I was twenty-five I married a bit of a hippy
which was sort of surprising to me
because I always thought I'd marry a punk.
She grew up harmonizing to Pure Prairie League
and dancing to Whipping Post barefoot in her
parent's backyard. It certainly rubbed off on me
because now I love Jonathan Edwards and Leo Kottke.

But now at thirty-five it's not unexpected to find her
skanking alone in the kitchen to The Dead Milkmen
or Big D and the Kids Table, and though our kids love
Aretha and Amos Lee, our four-year old has a particular
affinity for Rancid, and our one-year old slam dances
off of the kitchen walls for Operation Ivy-

and when she came home from daycare with teeth
marks in her arm filled in with a dark blue bruise
and my wife quietly and secretly threatened to bite
the less than two-year-old perpetrator I knew
for sure that I'm surrounded by punk rock girls
and dreams do come true.

Nicole Winters

meet me in Arizona

where ponderosas tower
& shroud the swollen moon

under the red rock,
  a different kind of cathedral,
across devil's bridge

& sleep under the milky way.
  at the end of the world
maybe the dust will settle

in winter, the south rim
cedar trees coated in snow
    we can sit at the precipice –

how majestic it must have been,
a river raging through sandstone
that left behind an oil painting

its layers ignite every evening
    at sundown
& maybe, in its midst,
we'll ignite, too.

Jessica Lowell Mason

Curator of Juvenalia

Who will be the curator of my golden era,
the time enfolded within time that seems
to dissipate while it blooms and looms
large, making shadows of the now,
who, when you go to the lighthouse,
that final time, when you are given over
wholly to a thiamine deficiency, will you
take with you— a trace of these adaptations,
of our retelling years into which we wove
the past into the present using only our lips,
our tongues, our larynxes,

our common hurt,

with an insistence neither of us questioned:
the past plays out like a record, not broken
but on repeat, and we play across tables,
repeated memories, between us, an archive
that is alive: the intimacy of readers
who know the story and want to hear it
again, word for word, cadence on cadence,
decrescendo to crescendo, for in each
repetition there is nova of knowledge,

a fissure of truth,

space dust in an interstellar puzzle
that cannot be put together, how it sits

before us, how we marvel at the movement
of the shapes of life we hold for a moment
and combine; it is not closure we seek,
but the right to write our own wisdom—
here, the past matters but only in segments,
and we relive each together,

this is ours,

an arrangement we compose and replay,
our song an inhale of what we refuse
to release; how many times do we return
to the stars together, to laughter not relinquished,
to our Nabokovian line, the way it cloaks us
in horror, a passage from Woolf: that communication

is health, is happiness,

is a girl telling of her adolescence;
your punchlines are reminders of lost treasures,
over dinner, inside envelopes covered in stickers
that read FRAGILE – but suggest tarnish:
tell me, is curation a life-line? were you giving me
the task of keeping you alive: if you go,
will I have failed? Will my past be denied
when you are no longer
there to verify it with repetitions?

You are the compulsion

to my obsession, the ovational audience
to my madness; some fulfill their duty
n the world clasped in a uniform, suspended
in the air over a wire, but I fulfilled mine
by giving you the storyteller in me, you call me

your little clown, the pieces of my childhood
I follow down halls in your mind, I laugh
my way into the gallery, eerily familiar,
brushed over with the pastels of sentimentality,

I hand you the particles

of remembrance so you can curate my life,
reprising my memories, but your mind
is going, slowly; I wait for the day
my memories will wander out of you,
the day you will reach a point of finality,
as when your mother found your father
pissing in the sink, mistaking it for a toilet,
what of me will defy the grasp of your intention,
what shape will my stories of hot gold
take when the crucible of laughter
cannot hold them, who will plunge
into that wreckage of juvenalia

where my heart waits

for its traveling companion, who will meld
with me into the mists of paradise, of misspellings,
who will remember what it was to live
as ghosts, to live where there were no walls.

www.ingramcontent.com/pod-product-compliance
Lightning Source LLC
Chambersburg PA
CBHW030311100526
44590CB00012B/586